C000094034

CELTIC
BLESSINGS

CELTIC BLESSINGS

PRAYERS FOR EVERY DAY

LAURENCE WAREING

BIRLINN

First published in Great Britain in 2020 by
Birlinn Ltd
West Newington House
10 Newington Road
Edinburgh
EH9 1QS

www.birlinn.co.uk

ISBN: 978 1 78027 569 7

Introductory material copyright © Laurence Wareing 2020
Illustrations copyright © Abigail Salvesen, 2020

The right of Laurence Wareing be identified as the
author of this work has been asserted by him in accordance
with the Copyright, Designs and Patents Act, 1988

All rights reserved. No part of this publication may
be reproduced, stored, or transmitted in any form,
or by any means, electronic, mechanical or photocopying,
recording or otherwise, without the express written
permission of the publisher.

British Library Cataloguing-in-Publication Data
A catalogue record for this book is available
on request from the British Library

Designed and typeset by Mark Blackadder

Printed and bound by Bell & Bain Ltd, Glasgow

For Helen,
companion on the way
and the best of partners

Contents

Acknowledgements

'Let us adore the Lord'; 'God be with me against all trouble'; 'Christ's cross over this face' from Gerard Murphy, *Early Irish Lyrics: eighth to twelfth century* (1998: Dublin, Four Courts Press), reproduced with permission.

'O helper of workers' from Thomas Owen Clancy and Gilbert Márkus, *Iona: The Earliest Poetry of a Celtic Monastery* (1995: Edinburgh, Edinburgh University Press), reproduced with permission of Edinburgh University Press through PLSclear.

'From this shield this day I call', trans. Fr Noel O'Donoghue, from James P. Mackey (ed.), *An Introduction to Celtic Christianity* (1989: Edinburgh, T&T Clark Ltd), reproduced by permission of T&T Clark Ltd, an imprint of Bloomsbury Publishing Plc.

It was a pleasure to be able to draw upon Roy Pinkerton's expertise for the translation of the 'Blessing of the three boys', and a reminder that Latin can be good fun over a coffee.

I've been increasingly grateful to be asked to

produce this companion volume to *Celtic Saints: Lives of the Holy Exiles*. For all the shadowy complexity of their provenance, these blessings do seem to express something of ancient lives now largely hidden by the mists of time. More importantly, reading them over repeatedly has turned me from a sceptic into an advocate of their enduring value and strength. Ann Crawford and Andrew Simmons have again been patient and helpful supporters through the compilation process. As always, Helen helped me get my thoughts into shape, as only she knows how.

Introduction

Running through the lives of the Celtic saints is a sense of connection with the natural world. It is what makes their stories, and writings associated with them, at once ancient and remote and yet also insistently relevant to our present-day lives.

The very few writings we have from the Celtic saints, together with the oral and written traditions that echo their priorities, are marked with vivid pictures of the world they inhabited. Sometimes just a single phrase evokes those aspects of nature they enjoyed but with which they also contended as they travelled, preached and took shelter. To our eyes and ears, these writings seem ancient partly because they focus on the basics of life that we nowadays summon with a flick of a switch or grab in haste in a local supermarket. At the same time, in their evocations of the world, they remind us of the very environments and natural events to which we are, again, turning our attention with ever-growing urgency.

By repeatedly evoking the presence of the sun or

the unpredictable power of the sea and by naming the important things in their lives (fire, cattle, four walls for shelter), the inhabitants of Celtic traditions offer memorable symbols for the world around us and of the fundamentals of life that we mostly take for granted. Their words help us reconnect with the earth from which we came and to which we will return. Within a single prayer, if we pause to breathe its meaning, we may experience simultaneously the mundane and the miraculous.

It is significant that these recurring symbols are so often wrapped in a blessing. Ian Bradley, a historian of Celtic Christianity, wonders whether this marked characteristic of the tradition 'reflects a pre-Christian Celtic sense of the power of the spoken word to heal and to harm'.

The summoning of such a power is not at all remote from our modern experience. A single tweet may arouse widespread anger and even spark violent responses. What the blessings included in this small volume remind us, though, is that the opposite may also be true: that a benediction or a word of grace contains the potential to establish the context or the frame of mind in which good and beneficial actions may take place. A blessing, in other words, is not just a perfunctory sentence or two at the close of a worship service or a bland greeting ('Good morning to you'). It embodies both the offering of hope and a call to action – to ourselves and to others. A blessing is transformative.

This collection is an abundant resource for everyone but, for those who have also read its companion volume, *Celtic Saints: Lives of the Holy Exiles*, it also endeavours to reflect themes and priorities that feature in those lives. In a few instances, this book draws on words attributed to the saints. Like many others, I have returned to Alexander Carmichael's influential collection of songs, prayers and poems from the Highlands and Islands of Scotland, *Carmina Gadelica*. I have also sought out other, older sources – the models for countless modern echoes and adaptations of the Celtic Blessing tradition. And the inclusion of 'The blessing of the three boys' from the seventh-century *Antiphonary of Bangor* is an important reminder that Celtic blessings have their roots as much in monastic liturgy as in the domestic prayers gathered from rural communities.

These older prayers hold up against newer imitations without need for any apology. With just a little explanation of less-familiar words and phrases, and especially when spoken out loud, they combine rhythm, balance and repetition with a directness of expression that chimes with our modern-day hopes and needs just as effectively as with the desires of those who first voiced them. As we speak the blessings quietly to ourselves, we may hold a picture in our minds of the island cottar who told Carmichael that he always recited his little journeying prayer whenever he left home *fo m'anail*, 'under my breath'. A blessing's influence is potent, he seems to suggest, however loudly or quietly you say it.

1 . Facing the day

In this first short group of invocations and poems, daily physical experience intertwines with an innate awareness of eternity; and the spoken word often alludes to a specific related action. Alexander Carmichael suggests, for example, that 'The Lustration' is an example of a prayer spoken while preparing to go to court, one which would involve praying in the early morning 'at a place where three streams met' – representing the three persons of the Christian Trinity (Father / Creator, Son and Holy Spirit).

It is the specific details that make these Celtic Blessings so approachable – such as references to 'my spouse and my children' or 'the eye that is in my head'. Even when they are at their most formal, as in 'The blessing of the three boys', the degree of detailed description is striking – 'Bless the Lord, every breath of wind . . . hoarfrost and snow . . . Lightning flashes . . . Praise and exalt him on high for ever.'

While wishing to avoid suggestions of pantheism (which erases the notion of a personal God of

Christian teaching and experience), we might never-theless say that, within the Celtic tradition, God and human experience of the natural world become almost as one. The sun is 'the eye of the great God'; or, in one ninth-century hymn, 'the white-waved sea' mirrors 'great bright Heaven':

Let us adore the Lord, maker of wondrous
works, great bright Heaven with its angels,
the white-waved sea on earth.

Throughout these prayers, there is an assumption of praise – from which all else follows. Praise of a divine presence opens the day and, with it, a desire for bless-ing both on the speaker and on others.

Glimpsing eternity

O God, who broughtest me from the rest of
   last night
Unto the joyous light of this day,
Be thou bringing me from the new light of this day
Unto the guiding light of eternity.
   Oh! from the new light of this day
   Unto the guiding light of eternity.

In the sun something divine

The eye of the great God,
The eye of the God of glory,
The eye of the King of hosts,
The eye of the King of the living
    Pouring upon us
        At each time and season,
    Pouring upon us
        Gently and generously.

    Glory to thee,
        Thou glorious sun.

    Glory to thee, thou sun,
        Face of the God of life.

The first wash of the day

*The Lustration**

I am bathing my face
In the mild rays of the sun,
As Mary bathed Christ
In the rich milk of Egypt.
Sweetness be in my mouth,
Wisdom be in my speech,
The love the fair Mary gave her Son
Be in the heart of all flesh for me.
The love of Christ in my breast,
The form of Christ protecting me,
There is not in sea nor on land
That can overcome the King of the Lord's Day.
The hand of Bride about my neck,
The hand of Mary about my breast,
The hand of Michael laving** me,
The hand of Christ saving me.

---

* a ceremonial washing, in this case prior to pursuing litigation,
see p. 15.
** washing.

Dressing for the day

Bless to me, O God,
　My soul and my body;
Bless to me, O God,
　My belief and my condition;

Bless to me, O God,
　My heart and my speech,
And bless to me, O God,
　The handling of my hand;

　Strength and busyness of morning,
Habit and temper of modesty,
Force and wisdom of thought,
And thine own path, O God of virtues,
　Till I go to sleep this night;

Thine own path, O God of virtues,
　Till I go to sleep this night.

For a spirit of blessing

Peace between neighbours,
Peace between kindred,
Peace between lovers,
    In love of the King of Life.

Peace between person and person,
Peace between wife and husband,
Peace between woman and children,
The peace of Christ about all peace.

Bless, O Christ, my face,
    Let my face bless everything.
Bless, O Christ, mine eye,
    Let mine eye bless all it sees.

For all that makes life meaningful

God, bless the world and all that is therein.
God, bless my spouse and my children,
God, bless the eye that is in my head,
And bless, O God, the handling of my hand;
What time I rise in the morning early,
What time I lie down late in bed,
  Bless my rising in the morning early,
  And in my lying down late in bed.

God, protect the house, and the household,
God, consecrate the children of the motherhood,
God, encompass the flocks and the young;
Be Thou after them and rending them,
What time the flocks ascend hill and wold,
What time I lie down to sleep,
  What time the flocks ascend hill and wold,*
  What time I lie down in peace to sleep.

---

* moor.

Blessing of the three boys*

Bless the Lord, all you works of the Lord: praise and
exalt him on high for ever.

Bless the Lord, you heavens: praise and exalt him on
high for ever.

Bless the Lord, angels of the Lord: praise and exalt
him on high for ever.

Bless the Lord, all the waters above the heavens:
praise and exalt him on high for ever.

---

*The three boys, Ananias, Azarias and Misael, are better known
to English speakers as Shadrach, Meshach and Abednego. The Old
Testament book of Daniel describes how they were thrown into a
fiery furnace by the Babylonian king Nebuchadnezzar for refusing
to betray their God and worship a golden image (Daniel, chapter
3).

This liturgical blessing was included in a seventh-century
Antiphonary (a book of sung chants for worship) created at
Comgall's monastery in Bangor, Northern Ireland. It was
preserved in the great library of Columbanus's foundation in
Bobbio in northern Italy. Translated from the Latin by Roy
Pinkerton with Laurence Wareing.

Bless the Lord, all you powers: praise and exalt him
on high for ever.

Bless the Lord, sun and moon: praise and exalt him
on high for ever.

Bless the Lord, stars of the heavens: praise and exalt
him on high for ever.

Bless the Lord, rain and dew: praise and exalt him
on high for ever.

Bless the Lord, every breath of wind: praise and
exalt him on high for ever.

Bless the Lord, fire and heat: praise and exalt him on
high for ever.

Bless the Lord, nights and days: praise and exalt him
on high for ever.

Bless the Lord, darkness and light: praise and exalt
him on high for ever.

Bless the Lord, winter and summer: praise and exalt
him on high for ever.

Bless the Lord, hoarfrost and snow: praise and exalt
him on high for ever.

Bless the Lord, lightning flashes and clouds: praise
and exalt him on high for ever.

Bless the Lord, O earth: praise and exalt him on
high for ever.

Bless the Lord, mountains and hills: praise and exalt
him on high for ever.

Bless the Lord, all things born of the earth: praise
and exalt him on high for ever.

Bless the Lord, seas and rivers: praise and exalt him
on high for ever.

Bless the Lord, springs of water: praise and exalt
him on high for ever.

Bless the Lord, sea monsters, and all that moves in
the waters: praise and exalt him on high for ever.

Bless the Lord, all the birds of the sky: praise and
exalt him on high for ever.

Bless the Lord, wild beasts and cattle: praise and
exalt him on high for ever.

Bless the Lord, people of Israel: praise and exalt him
on high for ever.

Bless the Lord, sons of men: praise and exalt him on
high for ever.

Bless the Lord, priests of the Lord: praise and exalt
him on high for ever.

Bless the Lord, servants of the Lord: praise and
exalt him on high for ever.

Bless the Lord, spirits and souls of the just: praise
and exalt him on high for ever.

Bless the Lord, saints and those with a humble
heart: praise and exalt him on high for ever.

Bless the Lord, Ananias, Azarias and Misael: praise
and exalt him on high for ever.

Let us bless the Lord, Father, Son and Holy Spirit:
let us praise and exalt him on high for ever.

2. For every task a blessing

The notion that 'any moment, any object, any job of work, can become a place for encounter with God' is attributed to the writer on Celtic Christian traditions, Esther De Waal. This idea is not peculiar to those traditions, of course – the seventeenth-century Carmelite lay brother Lawrence of the Resurrection, for example, wrote of encountering God through kitchen chores or repairing sandals. Nevertheless, the Celtic blessings and prayers that focus on everyday tasks speak unquestioningly of their sacredness.

The saints are always close at hand, not least Brigid, or 'Bride', a young woman whose life is unconstrained by the usual limitations or boundaries of human existence. She is said to have been born on the very threshold of her mother's home, literally in a 'liminal space'. Multiple legends of Brigid present the divine vividly alive in the mundane. This is imaginatively expressive of a thinness between earth and heaven. In these prayers, she is present, as 'calm Bride of the white combs'*, in the blessing of a cow and in a charm to heal a sprain – more than a minor inconvenience when it is your horse, your livelihood, that has suffered the injury. And, like Brigid herself, these blessings straddle the pre-Christian and the Christian, able to name Saint Columba and the druid Coivi in the same breath.

There is often an important metaphor shining within the evocation of an everyday task. In the Bathing Prayer, washing is far more than just a functional act. Its rhythms offer space to acknowledge the goodness inherent within the basics of living, and it concludes with a prayer that matches a threefold action with the three persons of the Christian Trinity. A trinitarian action is implied by many Celtic blessings, for example in the blessing of the kindling ('I will kindle my fire this morning'). The kindling itself is the vital 'pilot light' on which the home's heating and cooking depends: a miracle of divine power. It is also a metaphor for divine influence on the heart, which leads to love of neighbour – friend and enemy alike.

The sequential rhythms of many of these blessings suggest a need to renew that divine power regularly,

---

* breaking waves or 'white horses'.

both mentally and physically. Discipline is implied, but this is not as arduous as it might sound. Though at their most ascetic, saints such as Columbanus appear to preach the presence of God to the exclusion of any earthly pleasure, in these prayers an instinctive acceptance of a meaningful life beyond the immediately tangible reveals a holistic interpretation of day-to-day actions that otherwise seem repetitively one-dimensional:

God in my life,
God in my lips,
God in my soul,
God in my heart.

The saints close at hand

I will raise the heart-fire
As Mary would.
The encirclement of Bride and of Mary
On the fire, and on the floor,
And on the household all.

Who are they on the bare floor?
John and Peter and Paul.
Who are they by my bed?
The lovely Bride and her Fosterling*
Who are those watching over my sleep?
The fair loving Mary and her Lamb.
Who is it that is close by me?
The King of the sun He himself it is.
Who is that at the back of my head?
The Son of Life without beginning, without time.

---

* St Brigid/Bride was said to be the midwife to Mary and foster
mother to Jesus.

Lighting a spark – in the home, in the heart

I will kindle my fire this morning
In presence of the holy angels of heaven,
In presence of Ariel of the loveliest form,
In presence of Uriel of the myriad charms,
Without malice, without jealousy, without envy,
Without fear, without terror of any one under
    the sun,
But the Holy Son of God to shield me.
    Without malice, without jealousy, without envy,
    Without fear, without terror of any one under
       the sun,
    But the Holy Son of God to shield me.

God, kindle Thou in my heart within
A flame of love to my neighbour,
To my foe, to my friend, to my kindred all,
To the brave, to the knave, to the thrall,*
O Son of the loveliest Mary,
From the lowliest thing that liveth,
To the Name that is highest of all.

---

* servant or captive.

Peat fire smooring prayer*

The sacred Three
To save,
To shield,
To surround
The hearth,
The house,
The household
This eve,
This night,
Oh! This eve,
This night,
And every night,
Each single night.
Amen.

* In *Carmina Gadelica*, Alexander Carmichael notes, 'peat is the
fuel of the Highlands and Islands' and describes one method of
smooring, the process in which fire is smothered overnight,
allowing the heat to be retained ready for rekindling in the
morning:

The embers are evenly spread on the hearth . . . and formed into a circle. This circle is then divided into three equal sections, a small boss being left in the middle. A peat is laid between each section, each peat touching the boss, which forms a common centre. The first peat is laid down in the name of the God of Life, the second in the name of the God of Peace, the third in the name of the God of Grace. The circle is then covered over with ashes sufficient to subdue but not to extinguish the fire, in the name of the Three of Light.

Bathing Prayer – for a share of good things

A palmful for thine age,
    A palmful for thy growth,
A palmful for thy throat,
    A flood for thine appetite.

For thy share of the dainty,
    Crowdie and kail;*
For thy share of the taking,
    Honey and warm milk.

For thy share of the supping,
    Whisked whey and milk-product;
For thy share of the spoil,
    With bow and with spear.

For thy share of the preparation,
    The yellow eggs of Easter;
For thy share of the treat,
    My treasure and my joy,

---

* crowdie – a soft cheese made from buttermilk or soured milk;
kail – a green leafed, cabbage-like plant.

For thy share of the feast
　　With gifts and with tribute;
For thy share of the treasure,
　　Pulset of my love.**

·　　·　　·

The part of thee that does not grow at dawn,
　　May it grow at eventide;
The part of thee that does not grow at night,
　　May it grow at ridge of middle-day.

　　The three palmfuls
　　Of the Secret Three,
　　To preserve thee
　　From every envy,
　　Evil eye and death;
　　The palmful of the God of Life,
　　The palmful of the Christ of Love,
　　The palmful of the Spirit of Peace,
　　　　　Triune
　　　　　Of Grace.

** from an Irish Gaelic expression meaning 'my darling, my love'.

The Meal
(extract)

Give us, O God, of the morning meal,
  Benefit to the body, the frame of the soul;
Give us, O God, of the seventh bread*,
  Enough for our need at evening close.

Give us, O God, of the honey-sweet foaming milk,
  The sap and milk of the fragrant farms,
And give us, O God, along with Thy sleep,
  Rest in the shade of Thy covenant Rock.

·   ·   ·

Be with us by day, be with us by night,
  Be with us by light and by dark,
In our lying down and in our rising up,
  In speech, in walk, in prayer.

---

* the root of silverweed, Brisgean ('brittle one' in Gaelic), was
known as 'seventh bread'. It was a staple in the Highlands and
Islands before the introduction of the potato. It might be boiled,
roasted, or dried and ground into meal for bread and porridge.

Milking Blessing

Columba will give to her progeny,
Coivi* the propitious will give to her grass,
My speckled heifer will give me her milk,
And her female calf before her.
    Ho my heifer! heifer! heifer!
    Ho my heifer! kindly, calm,
    My heifer gentle, gentle, beloved,
        Thou are the love of thy mother.

Seest yonder thriving bramble bush
And the other bush glossy with brambles,
Such like is my fox-coloured heifer,
And her female calf before her.
    Ho my heifer! –

The calm Bride of the white combs
Will give to my loved heifer the lustre of the swan,
While the loving Mary, of the combs of honey,
Will give to her the mottle of the heather hen.
    Ho my heifer! –

---

* Coivi was a druid in pre-Christian tradition.

Charm of the sprain

Bride went out
In the morning early
With a pair of horses;
One broke his leg,
With much ado,
That was apart,
She put bone to bone,
She put flesh to flesh,
She put sinew to sinew,
She put vein to vein;
As she healed that
May I heal this.

Herdman Night (Am Buachaille)

'Night is a good herdman; he brings all creatures home.'
(Gaelic proverb)

Horo-i Horo-i Horo-i*
The sea-mew cries
Horo-i Horo-i Horo-i,
Sends Master Day his thralls to sea.

Horo-i Horo-i Horo-i,
pull strong lads,
Horo-i Horo-i Horo-i,
far out to sea.

---

* 'Horo-i' suggests the characteristic cry of the oyster catcher,
said to be St Bride's 'servant bird', though 'sea-mew' may refer to
the common gull.

As the early-twentieth-century song collector Kenneth
Macleod says, this song/blessing speaks of a community whose
rhythm is set by hours of daylight and darkness, when the men
('in thrall' to Master Day) go out to sea at dawn and hope to
return safely for nightfall. 'Night, the good herdman, bringeth all
creatures home, the men from the sea, the women from the
field.'

Horo-i Horo-i Horo-i
St Bride's Bird cries
Horo-i Horo-i Horo-i
Calls Herdman Night his children home.

Horo-i, pull strong lads, Horo-i
God speed you home.

Encircled by the Divine

God to enfold me,
God to surround me,
God in my speaking,
God in my thinking.

God in my sleeping,
God in my waking,
God in my watching,
God in my hoping.

God in my life,
God in my lips,
God in my soul,
God in my heart.

God in my sufficing,
God in my slumber,
God in mine ever-living soul,
God in mine eternity.

3. Prayers on the way

It is not at all surprising that blessings for safe travel are especially numerous among prayers of the Celtic traditions. Pilgrimage and a commitment to leaving home were significant features of the way of life adopted by most Celtic saints. Yet, even without that spiritual model, the challenges of sea crossings or making journeys across rural landscapes would have aroused real concerns and inspired hope-filled prayer. We are repeatedly made aware of mountain corries, dense forests, rugged hills and marshy sloughs.

Though modern travel is a very different experience in most parts of the world, perhaps there are hints of these ancient blessings in the charms and medallions hanging from the rear-view mirrors of cars and taxis. There is great joy to be had in the experience of travel (as Kenneth Macleod's 'Sea joy' reminds us) but, even today, there is often some more or less significant risk in embracing the wider world beyond our safe haven.

The intense blessing that opens this section ('Be

the great God between thy two shoulders') evokes perhaps the desperation of young Columbanus's mother. Having failed to prevent her boy from leaving home to embark on a radical act of self-purification, never to return, we may imagine her left in the doorway to watch him passing beyond view. He, meanwhile, filled with youthful determination, would have desired a complementary blessing:

Bless to me the thing
    Whereon is set my mind,
Bless to me the thing
    Whereon is set my love

It is an attitude that echoes strongly the demands made by Jesus in the Gospel of Luke: 'No one who puts a hand to the plough and looks back is fit for service in the kingdom of God.' (Luke 9:62)

While many of these prayers are rooted in the natural world – with all its stumbling blocks – symbolic meanings, as ever, lie close to hand. For example, 'Columba's herding' urges a divine watcher to protect the speaker's cattle 'from loch and from downfall', but there is also something universal about the closing petition: 'the peace of Columba be yours in the grazing . . . And may you return home safe-guarded'. Similarly, the petition that begins 'Be Thou a smooth way before me' recalls the teaching of Columbanus that human existence is a preparatory journey: 'the way that leads to life but not life itself'.

A mother's prayer and plea

Be the great God between thy two shoulders
To protect thee in thy going and in thy coming,
Be the Son of the Virgin Mary near thine heart,
And be the perfect Spirit upon thee pouring –
Oh, the perfect Spirit upon thee pouring!

All-round protection

The love and affection of heaven be to you,
The love and affection of the saints be to you,
The love and affection of the angels be to you,
The love and affection of the sun be to you,
The love and affection of the moon be to you,
    Each day and night of your lives,
      To keep you from haters, to keep you from
        harmers,
        to keep you from oppressors.

Journey Blessing*

Bless to me, O God,
    The earth beneath my foot,
Bless to me, O God,
    The path whereon I go;
Bless to me, O God,
    The thing of my desire;
        Thou Evermore of evermore,
    Bless Thou to me my rest.

Bless to me the thing
    Whereon is set my mind,
Bless to me the thing
    Whereon is set my love;
Bless to me the thing
    Whereon is set my hope;
        O Thou King of kings
    Bless Thou to me mine eye!

---

* See p. 14.

Blessing of the Road

May the hills lie low,
May the sloughs* fill up
In thy way.

May all the evil sleep,
May all good awake,
In thy way.

---

* soft, muddy ground or bog that makes the path impassable,
here evoking a peaty landscape.

Prayer for travelling

Life be in my speech,
Sense in what I say,
The bloom of cherries on my lips
Till I come back again.

The love Christ Jesus gave
Be filling every heart for me,
The love Christ Jesus gave
Filling me for every one.

Traversing corries, traversing forests,
Traversing valleys long and wild.
The fair white Mary still uphold me,
The Shepherd Jesu be my shield,
The fair white Mary still uphold me,
The Shepherd Jesu be my shield.

In the name of Finian*

A tower of gold over every sea-plain:
he will give a hand to help my soul,
Findian the fair, a loveable root,
of vast Clonard.

---

* Finian (here named 'Findian') was the founder of the major
monastic settlement at Clonard in Ireland.

50

Columba's path

Attributed to St Columba

The path I walk, Christ walks it.
May the land in which I am be without sorrow.
May the Trinity protect me whenever I stray,
Father, Son and Holy Spirit.

Bright Angels walk with me – dear presence – in
    every dealing.
In every dealing I pray them that no one's poison
    may reach me.
The ninefold people of heaven of holy cloud,
the tenth force of the stout earth.*
Favourable company, they come with me,
so that the Lord may not be angry with me.

May I arrive at every place, may I return home;
may the way in which I spend be a way without loss.
May every path before me be smooth,
man, woman and child welcome me.

---

* possibly referring to a hierarchy of angelic beings, each assigned
special responsibilities.

A truly good journey!
Well does the fair Lord show us a course, a path.

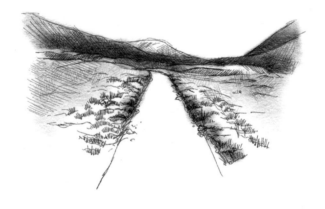

Columba's Herding

May the herding of Columba
Encompass you going and returning,
Encompass you in strath and on ridge
    And on the edge of each rough region;

May it keep you from pit and from mire,
Keep you from hill and from crag,
Keep you from loch and from downfall,
    Each evening and each darkling;

May it keep you from the mean destroyer,
Keep you from the mischievous niggard,*
Keep you from the mishap of bar-stumbling
    And from the untoward fays.**

The peace of Columba be yours in the grazing,
    The peace of Brigit be yours in the grazing,
The peace of Mary be yours in the grazing,
    And may you return home safe-guarded.

---

* a mean, stingy person.
** malign fairies or spirits.

The driving
(extracts)*

The protection of Odhran the dun** be yours,
the protection of Brigit the nurse be yours,
the protection of Mary the Virgin be yours
    in marshes and in rocky ground,
    in marshes and in rocky ground.

The sanctuary of Colum Cille be yours,
the sanctuary of Maol Ruibhe be yours,
the sanctuary of the milking Maid be yours
    to seek you and search for you,
    to seek you and search for you.

The shield of the King of Fiann*** be yours,
the shield of the King of the sun be yours,
the shield of the King of the stars be yours
    in jeopardy and distress,
    in jeopardy and distress.

---

* one of many similar blessings on cattle and livestock, reflecting
a pragmatic awareness of the particular dangers they might face.
** St Odhran ('Oran') was a companion of Columba (Colum
Cille), buried next to Iona Abbey.
*** the Fianna were small bands of warriors in Irish mythology.

A petition

Be Thou a smooth way before me,
Be Thou a guiding star above me,
Be Thou a keen eye behind me,
This day, this night, for ever.

I am weary, and I am forlorn,
Lead Thou me to the land of the angels;
Methinks it were time I went for a space
To the court of Christ, to the peace of the heavens.

If only Thou, O God of my life,
Be at peace with me, be my support,
Be to me as a star, be to me as a helm,
From my lying down in peace to my rising anew.

Barra fishers' sea prayer and Sea joy*

Sea prayer (Urnuigh Mhara)

On rise o' wave or on steep o' hill
May thy hand sain** and save us still.
On back of wave or on slop o' brae,
Be thou our helper and guide, we pray.
Be our guide we pray.

---

* a prayer from *Carmina Gadelica* bookending Kenneth Macleod's song, 'Sea Joy'. He writes:

> Now and again, in harvest time, when there is a light breeze, and the sea is on the swell, more from the joy of it than from evil intent, and the sun has the rich glow of sea-tangle, St Bride's Bird, the oyster catcher, may be seen, proud and graceful, rising and falling with the rising and falling waves. On such an evening the Isle-folk say that Bride (Breedja) is in laughter.

** bless with the sign of a cross.

Sea joy

Skies to westward,
Ho ee o heu-o,
Shine like sea tangle,
Ho ee o, heu-o,
Breedja's in laughter rare,*
Fal 'you' o ho ho
Ho ee o heu-o.

All I long for,
Ho ee o heu-o,
Through the blue sea-deeps,
Ho ee o heu-o,
Outsails my longing far,
Fal 'you' o ho ho
Ho ee o heu-o.

Joy of seeking,
Ho ee o heu-o,
Joy of n'er finding,
Ho ee o heu-o,
Breedja's in laughter rare,
Fal 'you' o ho ho
Ho ee o heu-o.

———————

* 'Breedja': St Bride as pronounced in the Gaelic.

Sea prayer

On rise o' wave or on steep o' brae,
Be thou our helper and guide, we pray.
Be our guide we pray.

St Columba's assurance

Attributed to St Columba

Alone with none but Thee, my God,
I journey on my way;
What need I fear when Thou art near,
Oh King of night and day?
More safe am I within Thy hand
Than if a host did round me stand.

With God at my back

(extract)

God and Jesus and the Holy Spirit
Be shielding and saving me,
As Three and as One,
By my knee, by my back, by my side,
    Each step of the stormy world.

Traditional Gaelic blessing

May the road rise up to meet you.
May the wind be always at your back.
May the sun shine warm upon your face;
the rains fall soft upon your fields and,
until we meet again,
may God hold you in the palm of His hand.

4. Ever-present dangers

Beginning with 'a prayer setting out on a journey', this section forms a natural progression from the theme of Prayers on the Way.

Seafaring, particularly across the perilous Irish Sea, was essential for the eastward drive of Celtic Christianity. It was also the means to a fishing livelihood, and ships and currachs facilitated communication, clan expansion, exploration, enemy invasion, exile and new beginnings. Yet for merchants, warriors and saints alike, to set out across the waves and face often harsh, unpredictable elements, was to touch eternity. Unsurprisingly, a number of miracles associated with the Celtic saints (Columba, Cainnech and Baldred, for instance) include prayers and actions to protect sailors in trouble at sea.

Two prayers here draw us on board the birlinns of the Macdonalds of Clanranald as they cross to Moidart on the British mainland. Another petition declares very simply that 'the sea is so wide, and my boat is so small': simple but not simplistic and, like most of the blessings here, with a symbolic depth applicable to the voids and unknowns of modern living.

Other threats and concerns are named, especially in the ninth-century petition to God to 'be with me against all trouble'. This prayer raises memories of those saints for whom present dangers were many and varied: the demons banished by Cuthbert and Aidan; rampant plague from which Columba and Ciannech fled but which probably killed Ciaran of Clonfort; and attacks from marauders, feared by Ebba and experienced by Patrick. Even the pain and incapacity caused by urinary infections gets a mention.

In this context, the 'lorica' prayers for protection, such as the four included here, suggest a good deal more than meaningless ritual and repetition. They gather together values and virtues as if putting on battle dress ('lorica' was the Latin for the armour worn by Roman soldiers). In the rhythmic naming of the saints, or of Christ and the perceived saving power of his crucifixion, they develop an oral intensity that gets under the skin of modern readers as much as for their first speakers.

A prayer setting out on a journey

I set the keeping of Christ about thee,
I send the guarding of God with thee,
To possess thee, to protect thee
From drowning, from danger, from loss.

The Gospel of the God of grace
Be from thy summit to thy sole;
The Gospel of Christ, King of salvation,
Be as a mantle to thy body.

Nor drowned be thou at sea
Nor slain be thou on land
Nor o'erborne be thou by man
Nor undone be thou by woman!

Dawn Prayer of the Clanranalds*
(extracts)

Fragrant maiden of the sea,
blessed art thou among women;

.　　.　　.

Let me beseech thy gentle Son
to whom thou gavest knee and suck
　　to be with us,
　　to be on watch,
　　to be awake;
to spread over us his sacred cowl**
from ray-light to ray-light,
from the golden-yellow ray of twilight
to the new-born white ray of dawn,
and through the dark and dangerous night
　　to succour us,

---

* A prayer 'which was wont to be chanted by the Macdonalds of
the Isles [of Clanranald], when crossing to their chiefs' main
territories', writes Kenneth Macleod. He offers the theory that
these lines are 'a corrupted survival of the old Celtic Church
Music, a link with Iona and St. Columba'.
* a loose hood, part of a monk's habit.

to guide us,
to shine on us
with the guidance and glory of the nine rays
of the Sun,
through seas and straits and narrows
until we come to Moidart***
and the Good Clanranald;
O until we come to Moidart
and the Good Clanranald.

*** a sea loch on Scotland's west coast.

The Birlinn of Clanranald, or Clanranald's Galley

(extracts)

Father of ocean,
Bless our birlinn,*
Sweep smooth the waves,
Our port draw nigh.
Bless all our mast hoops,
Our ropes and halyards,
May no evil e'er to them come nigh.

Speed our birlinn black and shapely,
Bulging sea glens piled before us,
Blinded by the spray of surges,
Watching well the briny storm-hills.

Hoist we our sail from Uist of wild geese,
Oars a-twisting – billows a-curling,
Thrust our galley hissing through sea glens,
Fireballs blazing high i' the rigging.

---

* a wooden vessel propelled by sail and oar.

Full the deep of crawling spectres,
Seals all torn and great sea monsters,
All a-howling, screeching, groaning,
'Drag us all aboard your birlinn'.

Drive the mountain monsters onward,
Pounding grey-backed swirling eddies,
Send the surge in sparkles skyward
Hoary-headed seas up-swelling.

Extracts from Alexander Macdonald's powerful sea-poem,
trans. Sheriff Nicholson.

Fisherman's prayer

Big Sea, Little Boat,
Dear God, be good to me;
The sea is so wide,
And my boat is so small.

St John's Wort and Figwort*

Plantlet of Columba,
without seeking, without searching,
plantlet of Columba,
under my arm for ever!

For luck of men,
For luck of means,
For luck of wish,
For luck of sheep,
For luck of goats,
For luck of birds,
For luck of fields,
For luck of shell-fish,
For luck of fish,
For luck of produce and kine,**

---

* Alexander Carmichael explains that St John's Wort was
associated with Columba, and with a tradition of secreting it, in
the case of men, under the left armpit. On the mainland, the
leaves and tubers of the figwort were known for their medicinal
properties, while on the islands the plant was believed to ward
off enchantment or ill luck, and ensure peace and prosperity.
** an archaic plural of 'cow'.

For luck of progeny and people,
For luck of battle and victory,
On land, on sea, on ocean,
Through the Three on high,
Through the Three a-nigh,
Through the Three eternal,
Plant of Columba,
I cull thee now,
    I cull thee now.

Adiutor laborantium*

Attributed to St Columba

O helper of workers,
ruler of all the good,
guard on the ramparts
and defender of the faithful,
who lift up the lowly
and crush the proud,**

---

* Clancy and Márkus (*Iona: The Earliest Poetry of a Celtic Monastery*)
note that 'the vulnerability of a sailor in a frail boat on the open
sea is an eloquent symbol of the Christian life and Irish writers
made full use of it. But the sea-voyage was clearly far more than a
literary device.' They quote the seventh-century Irish poet and
monk Beccán mac Luigdech who, in his 'Last Verses', vividly
imagines the missionary journey of Columba from Ireland:

> 'In scores of curraghs with an army of wretches he
> crossed the long-haired sea.
>
> .   .   .
>
> He crossed the wave-strewn wild region, foam-flecked,
> seal-filled, savage, bounding, seething, white-tipped,
> pleasing, doleful.'

** compare with the Magnificat of Mary in the Gospel of Luke
1:46–56.

ruler of the faithful,
enemy of the impenitent,
judge of all judges,
who punish those who err,
pure life of the living,
light and Father of lights
shining with great light,
denying to none of the hopeful
your strength and help,
I beg that me, a little man
trembling and most wretched,
rowing through the infinite storm
of this age,
Christ may draw after Him to the lofty
most beautiful heaven of life
. . . an unending
holy hymn forever.

For protection against all trouble

God be with me against all trouble, noble Trinity
    which is one, Father, Son, and Holy Spirit.

The bright holy King of the Sun, who is more beau-
    tiful than anything to which we have a right, is a
    wondrous refuge for me against the host of black
    demons.

The Father, the Son, the glorious Holy Spirit, may
    these three protect me against all plague-bearing
    clouds.

Against violent or sudden death, against all
    brigands' plunderings, may great Jesus guard me
    against dysury.*

Against demons at any time is the Son of God who
    protects me, against disease, against wounding,
    against thunder and fire.

---

* difficult or painful urination.

Against grievous oppression and all other cruelty
may the Son of Mary graciously bless my body.

.   .   .

May God be ever present to guard me, glorious
Lord of angels, so that when he comes to claim
the deposit received from Him he may find it
safe.

May the King guard me; may he aid me always; may
I be at every need beneath the protection of
God's hand.

A cross of protection*

Christ's cross over this face, and thus over my ear.
Christ's cross over this eye. Christ's cross over this
nose.

Christ's cross over this mouth. Christ's cross over
this throat. Christ's cross over the back of this
head. Christ's cross over this side.

Christ's cross over this belly (so is it fitting). Christ's
cross over this lower belly. Christ's cross over
this back.

Christ's cross over my arms from my shoulders to
my hands. Christ's cross over my thighs. Christ's
cross over my legs.

---

* An early (tenth-century?) prayer for protection. A traditional
attribution to Columba is 'linguistically impossible' according to
Gerard Murphy. He writes that the prayer's 'enumeration of the
parts of the body . . . bears a striking resemblance to Mugrón's
Crosradach' (Mugrón being one of Columba's successors). Lorica-
type prayers suggest the influence of Irish and Welsh charms, but
also St Paul's metaphor of the armour of God to combat evil (e.g.
Ephesians 6:14–18). St Patrick's Breastplate is perhaps the most
well-known example (p. 82).

Christ's cross to accompany me before me. Christ's cross to accompany me behind me. Christ's cross to meet every difficulty both on hollow and hill.

Christ's cross eastward facing me. Christ's cross back towards the sunset. In the north, in the south unceasingly may Christ's cross straightway be.

Christ's cross over my teeth lest injury or harm come to me. Christ's cross over my stomach. Christ's cross over my heart.

Christ's cross up to broad Heaven. Christ's cross down to earth. Let no evil or hurt come to my body or soul.

Christ's cross over me as I sit. Christ's cross over me as I lie. Christ's cross be all my strength till we reach the King of Heaven.

Christ's cross over my community. Christ's cross over my church. Christ's cross in the next world; Christ's cross in this.

From the top of my head to the nail of my foot, O
   Christ, against every danger I trust in the
   protection of thy cross.

Till the day of my death, before going into this clay, I
   shall draw without . . . Christ's cross over this
   face.

Gifts of the saints

May Christ and his Saints stand between you
and harm.
Mary and her Son.
Patrick with his staff.
Martin with his mantle.
Brigid with her veil.
Michael with his shield.
And God over all with his strong right hand.

Alexander's Breastplate[*]

On the face of the earth his equal was not born,
Three persons of God, one Son gentle, strong
    Trinity.
Son of the Godhead, Son of the Manhood, one son
    wonderful.
Son of God, a fortress, Son of the blessed Mary, a
    good son to see.
Great his destiny, great God supreme, a glorious
    portion.
Of the race of Adam and Abraham he was born.
Of the race of the Lord, a portion of the eloquent
    host, was he born.
He brought by a word the blind and deaf from every
    ailment.
A people gluttonous, vain, iniquitous, vile,
    perverse,
We have risen against[**] the Trinity, after
    redemption,

---

[*] named because it is placed between two poems about
Alexander the Great in the Welsh *Book of Taliesin* XXVII.
[**] toward.

The Cross of Christ clearly, a breastplate gleaming
against every ailment.
Against every hardship may it be certainly a city of
protection.

St Patrick's Breastplate

(extracts)*

For my shield this day I call:
A mighty power:
The Holy Trinity!
Affirming threeness,
Confessing oneness,
In the making of all
Through love . . .

For my shield this day I call:
Christ's power in his coming
and in his baptising,
Christ's power in his dying
On the cross, his arising
from the tomb, his ascending;
Christ's power in his coming
for judgment and ending.

.   .   .

---

* trans. Fr Noel O'Donoghue (James P. Mackey ed.
An Introduction to Celtic Christianity) See note to 'A cross of
protection', p. 76.

For my shield this day I call:
Heaven's might,
Sun's brightness,
Moon's whiteness,
Fire's glory,
Lightning's swiftness,
Wind's wildness,
Ocean's depth,
Earth's solidity,
Rock's immobility.

This day I call to me;
God's strength to direct me,
God's power to sustain me,
God's wisdom to guide me,
God's vision to light me,
God's ear to my hearing,
God's word to my speaking,
God's hand to uphold me,
God's pathway before me,
God's shield to protect me,
God's legions to save me:
from snares of the demons,
from evil enticements,
from failings of nature,
from one man or many

that seek to destroy me,
anear or afar.

Be Christ this day my protector;
against poison and burning,
against drowning and wounding,
through reward wide and plenty . . .

Christ beside me, Christ before me;
Christ behind me, Christ within me;
Christ beneath me, Christ above me;
Christ to right of me, Christ to left of me;
Christ in my lying, my sitting, my rising;
Christ in heart of all who know me,
Christ on tongue of all who meet me,
Christ in eye of all who see me,
Christ in ear of all who hear me.

For my shield this day I call
a mighty power:
the Holy Trinity!
affirming threeness,
confessing oneness
in the making of all –
through love . . .

5. Hope in the darkness

Blessings for the close of day mirror those for the day's dawn. Lying down and rising up are part of a recurring rhythm to which, nowadays, we barely give a second thought. Or perhaps the stabilising rhythm is lost altogether, broken down by work shift patterns, 24-hour news and shopping, the ceaseless buzz of social media, and an inability for many of us to create consistent, meaningful space for ourselves and our relationships.

The blessings in this closing section recall the glimpses of eternity with which the day began, and the desire for peace between neighbours, between kindred, and between lovers (p. 21). Here, there are blessings for self and one's home, but generous blessings for others also: 'My own blessing be with you . . . And with your children, With you and with your children'.

Again, the Christian Trinity is a recurring presence. This offers a balance in the way the Divine is named and understood (always a sense of 'both *and*').

But the trinitarian pattern also informs, and is part and parcel of, a desire for balance and rhythm in everyday life. Nowhere is that balance and rhythm more evident than on the shoreline – the shore from which many a sea journey has been launched, with all the challenges and terrors that might entail, but where the constant tidal movement also offers an eternal image of divine constancy and flexibility, of parameters and possibilities:

> With the ebb
> With the flow,
> O Thou Triune
> Of grace!

God with me lying down

God with me lying down,
God with me rising up,
God with me in each ray of light,
Nor I a ray of joy without him,
    Nor one ray without him.

Christ with me sleeping,
Christ with me waking,
Christ with me watching,
    Each day and night.

God with me protecting,
The Lord with me directing,
The Spirit with me strengthening,
For ever and for evermore,
    Ever and evermore, Amen.
    Chief of chiefs, Amen.

The four corners of the house

The peace of God, the peace of men,
The peace of Columba kindly,
The peace of Mary mild, the loving,
The peace of Christ, King of tenderness,
    The peace of Christ, King of tenderness.

Be upon each window, upon each door,
Upon each hole that lets in light.
Upon the four corners of my house,
Upon the four corners of my bed,
    Upon the four corners of my bed.

Upon each thing my eye takes in,
Upon each thing my mouth takes in,
Upon my body that is of earth
And upon my soul that came from on high,
    Upon my body that is of earth
    And upon my soul that came from on high.

Deep peace*

Deep peace I breathe into you,
O weariness, here:
O ache, here!
Deep peace, a soft white dove to you;
Deep peace, a quiet rain to you;
Deep peace, an ebbing wave to you!
Deep peace, red wind of the east from you;
Deep peace, grey wind of the west to you;
Deep peace, dark wind of the north from you;
Deep peace, blue wind of the south to you!
Deep peace, pure red of the flame to you;
Deep peace, pure white of the moon to you;
Deep peace, pure green of the grass to you;
Deep peace, pure brown of the earth to you;
Deep peace, pure grey of the dew to you;
Deep peace, pure blue of the sky to you!
Deep peace of the running wave to you,

---

* from *The Dominion of Dreams* (1899) by William Sharp, writing
as Fiona Macleod. In the novel, the prayer brings about the
healing of a man who has lost his mind. With the words, 'O
weariness, here: O ache, here!' the speaker touches first his brow
and then his heart.

Deep peace of the flowing air to you,
Deep peace of the quiet earth to you,
Deep peace of the sleeping stones to you!
Deep peace of the Yellow Shepherd to you,
Deep peace of the Wandering Shepherdess to you,
Deep peace of the Flock of Stars to you,
Deep peace from the Son of Peace to you,
Deep peace from the heart of Mary to you,
And from Briget* of the Mantle
Deep peace, deep peace!
And with the kindness too of the Haughty Father,
Peace!
In the name of the Three who are One,
Peace! And by the will of the King of the Elements,
Peace! Peace!

---

* St Brigid.

A personal blessing on others

My own blessing be with you,
The blessing of God be with you,
The blessing of the Spirit be with you
    And with your children,
        With you and with your children.

My own blessing be with you,
The blessing of God be with you,
The blessing of saints be with you,
    And the peace of the life eternal,
    Unto the peace of the life eternal.

Surrounded by God

God to enfold me,
God to surround me,
God in my speaking,
God in my thinking.

God in my sleeping,
God in my waking,
God in my watching,
God in my hoping.

God in my life,
God in my lips,
God in my soul,
God in my heart.

God in my sufficing,
God in my slumber,
God in mine ever-living soul,
God in mine eternity.

With the ebb and flow

As it was,
As it is,
As it shall be
Evermore,
O Thou Triune
Of grace!
With the ebb
With the flow,
O Thou Triune
Of grace!
With the ebb
With the flow.

Sources

Bradley, I., *Colonies of Heaven: Celtic Models for Today's Church* (2000: London, Darton, Longman and Todd Ltd)

Bradley, I., *Following the Celtic Way: A New Assessment of Celtic Christianity* (2018: London, Darton, Longman and Todd Ltd)

Carmichael, A., *Carmina Gadelica*, vols 1–4 (1900–41: Edinburgh, Oliver and Boyd)

Clancy, T.O. and Gilbert Márkus, *Iona: The Earliest Poetry of a Celtic Monastery* (1995: Edinburgh, Edinburgh University Press)

Kennedy-Fraser, M. and Kenneth Macleod, eds, *Songs of the Hebrides*, vols 1–3 (1909–21: London, Boosey & Co.)

Mackey, J.P., ed., *An Introduction to Celtic Christianity* (1989: Edinburgh, T&T Clark Ltd)

Macleod, F. (William Sharp) *The Dominion of Dreams* (1899: London, Archibald Constable and Co.)

Macleod, K., *The Road to the Isles* (1927: Edinburgh, Robert Grant & Son)

Macquarrie, A., ed., *Legends of Scottish Saints: Readings, Hymns and Prayers for the Commemorations of Scottish Saints in the Aberdeen Breviary* (2012: Dublin, Four Courts Press)

Mould, D.P., *The Irish Saints* (1964: Dublin, Clonmore and Reynolds Ltd)

Murphy, G., trans. & ed., *Early Irish Lyrics: Eighth to Twelfth Century* (1998: Dublin, Four Courts Press)

Skene, William F., *The Four Ancient Books of Wales* (1868: Edinburgh, Edmonston and Douglas)

www.acollectionofprayers.com

www.faithandworship.com/Celtic_Blessings_and_Prayers.htm

www.visitdunkeld.com/celtic-blessing-prayers.htm